PRAISE FOR
OF BLOOD AND RIVERS

"Michael Delp is our most eloquent and innovative celebrant of rivers, but I was not prepared for the raw power of these elegies. Here is language condensed to its sinews and heart tissue—poems with the blood and flesh of dreams still clinging to them. They tell us how to live with 'the fist . . . inside the scar,' that loneliness has 'the memory of pure joy pounding on the door,' that grief 'is not shed like a skin; you carry it a lifetime.' I've always kept Mike Delp's books on the same shelf as Jim Harrison and Mary Oliver. *Of Blood and Rivers* gets a shelf of its own."

—JERRY DENNIS, author of *Mornings at Jack Pine* and *Up North in Michigan*

"What if a river could speak? If its meanderings cutting through the black earth were letters? Michael Delp is such a river, weaving poems out of tributaries, smoke, and fishing line. He rewrites the lyric impulse into elegiac prose poems small as stones on the riverbed—not as tombs, but precise epiphanies."

—SEAN THOMAS DOUGHERTY, author of *Death Prefers the Minor Keys*

"Michael Delp, the mad angler and the river god, finds that each surface ripple, click of pebbles, or flash of fish has equivalents in the soul's own currents. Channeling Snyder, Bly, Han Shan, Harrison, and Kinnell, he creates meandering, mystical meditations on grief and joy, astonishment and anger, repose and discovery, and love and loss, capturing the susurrus of the self always searching, swimming, rising, and hooking the earthbound wonder of our days."

—Norm Wheeler, Leelanau School Beach Bard

"I read these grief-born meditations with pleasure, which seems like an odd way to respond to anguish and longing. The pleasure comes from being in the presence of unapologetic humanity and devotion, especially to words. Enacting for readers a deep dive into one's own consciousness while dipping one hand into a beloved river and the other into the stars feels generous and way-making. At some moments along the way I thought of Judith Minty's *Yellow Dog Journal*; at some others, Rilke's *Duino Elegies*. We are lucky indeed to have Michael Delp's remarkable poem-prayers."

—Alison Swan, author of *River Mouth* and *A Fine Canopy* (Wayne State University Press)

"Michael Delp's *Of Blood and Rivers* is a book of wonders: prayers to be absorbed by the natural world, praying that world into the poems, which are themselves prayers that this world may continue. These are poems that will absorb your attention, awaken your heart, and maybe take your breath away."

—Dan Gerber

"What can I say about these words that they don't say for themselves? They are arresting, surprising, piercing, chilling, honest, and clear. They roll on as you turn the pages, much like their subjects roll on. Each burst on the page adds something: an accretion, a search for joy, the authentic self. This is the voice of someone struggling to become new in the oldest way possible: through the utterance of air passing over flesh and into the universe. This is Michael Delp's best book yet."

—Doug Stanton, #1 *New York Times* bestselling author

"This book is part blood transfusion, part means of transport to the outer dark of the cosmos. In that sense it is both lifesaving and soul-expanding. Who knew that grief could carry one so mortally far away from home, or that the griever could find his way back home by following the sound of the river? I read this book and came back to life."

—Chris Dombrowski, author of *Body of Water*

OF BLOOD AND RIVERS

MADE IN MICHIGAN
WRITERS SERIES

SERIES EDITORS

Natalie Bakopoulos
Nandi Comer
Desiree Cooper
Frances Kai-Hwa Wang

ASSOCIATE EDITOR, POETRY

Kamelya Omayma Youssef

A complete listing of the books in this series can be found online at wsupress.wayne.edu.

OF BLOOD AND RIVERS

A BOOK OF ELEGIES

MICHAEL DELP

Afterword by Nick Bozanic

WAYNE STATE UNIVERSITY PRESS
DETROIT

ISBN 9780814353417 (paperback)
ISBN 9780814353424 (ebook)

Library of Congress Control Number: 2026935376

Cover illustration and design by Lindsey Cleworth.

Publication of this book was made possible by a generous gift from The Meijer Foundation.

Some of these poems have appeared in *Convivium Magazine* and a small chapbook titled *Seven River Prayers* from St Brigid Press, and most of them are housed in the author's social media account.

Wayne State University Press rests on Waawiyaataanong, also referred to as Detroit, the ancestral and contemporary homeland of the Three Fires Confederacy. These sovereign lands were granted by the Ojibwe, Odawa, Potawatomi, and Wyandot Nations, in 1807, through the Treaty of Detroit. Wayne State University Press affirms Indigenous sovereignty and honors all tribes with a connection to Detroit. With our Native neighbors, the press works to advance educational equity and promote a better future for the earth and all people.

Wayne State University Press
Leonard N. Simons Building
4809 Woodward Avenue
Detroit, Michigan 48201-1309

Visit us online at wsupress.wayne.edu.

For Claudia, 1950–2022

The love of this life and the next one . . .

If I could, I would yield to the softest thing in the universe, the path of least resistance, every step downhill and away, not even stopping to look back . . . this life's wounded mysteries, why thousands of words never left my tongue, why I sought so much outside the chamber of the human heart, why the sound of my prayers comes back echoing, desiring these poems to be part dance, part madness, sometimes locked in the earth, sometimes carried by rivers, sometimes drifting the sky.

Up in the clearing, five wild dogs circling, bloody
snouts and smoke coming from black holes in the
snow, the full moon making my shadow long and
lean, nothing to do but offer up dog words mixed
with blood . . . who cares what happens next,
what the body will do as it is torn apart, the end
of songs, poems, my flesh left as a torn prayer flag,
the beginning of the long journey of spirit into
the sky cistern, which holds a darker blood.

Somehow I was granted the choice between the exploding supernova and the collapsed star and, of course, chose the dark one . . . light falling toward itself to a single point where all questions cease and the sky does not exist except in memory, which falls in on itself beyond a childhood in the '50s, all the streetlights suddenly gone out, trying to find vanished porches, my grandmother who reaches for a light switch, which is always vanishing.

Sometimes I am able to hold back the river, stop
time, watch the debris pile up, some real, most
of it imagined, noticing how the worst clumps
of regret somehow find each other and move
closer, then through me . . . that fine thread no
heavier than spider silk unravels out of me, and
soon there is nothing left but sinew, a few shreds
of heart tissue, waving not like a flag under water,
but exactly as a shred, left over from something
long gone.

Already a morning of circling raptors, their
talons out dragging the air, every now and then
that deliberate plummet to the ground, then
sometimes back up into a tree to dismantle a
small life or sometimes rushing back up to ride
another swirling thermal . . . and I think of myself
up there, almost weightless, fueled only by desire
for what walks the ground on two legs, so sure I
could easily open those beautiful poems floating
like bright moons just under her skin.

Another Lament for Jim Harrison

Of course, we die as all have done and will, the
days burn down to ash and sooner or later all of
this will disappear into a beautiful, final silence,
the universe and every other universe stopped,
dead . . . so in your honor I made a pen and
heated ink from river water, cedar sap, and of
course blood, then wrote this poem, built a small
pyre out of scavenged beaver sticks, placed the pen
ever so carefully pointing north, stepped back and
let it flare into the sweet, early evening, the ink
going last, earth to fire, vapor, then no light left in
the fire, knowing I would come back in a dream
to devour the ash.

Carpe diem shifts on me every day, and I prowl water talking to ghosts, myself at eight years old, wanting to have him hold me underwater for one last look at a blue sky, seized by days, hundreds of them sluicing away, the air thick with all of those lovely moans that have somehow escaped me . . . always looking for the saddled horse, the one I might ride into town after the apocalypse to burn poems into the foreheads of those who didn't see it coming.

Every bygone I let go, tossed skyward and then down into the river, becomes a phantom before it hits the water, as if it never existed, the air filled with the tiniest parts of moments . . . my head is a pen, the day something to be written down, as if to be recalled, the dark moments on each page caught, then abandoned, then the head takes in more: evening, night, black sky. The stars become the holes left by what is lost.

The full moon coming, merging with the solstice, an amber light caused, we are told, by that same light seeping through high humidity, and the wind bending trees above me, every old trail out of the past covered over by deadfall . . . the river roils and churns in front of me, silver and black, so I lean in, dip my head into cold water, speak the first words of a poem, instantly lost to the current, the river becoming a perfect book, poem gone as soon as it is spoken, raising no questions, the beauty of no answers.

Who needs a reminder of the weight of time, the
full moon on the solstice not to be seen again for
seventy years, so I suppose I will see a few ghosts
sitting under the half-lit cedars tonight tracking it
across the sky, no talking, barely whispers, hoping
for at least one to turn back over his shoulder,
pass along the map to get out of here . . . "gone"
comes off the tongue too often these days, the
heart cooling down like a coal dropped into water,
the sizzle forgotten immediately, the silences
upon silences of epochs coming endlessly over an
endless horizon, maybe to come back as bird of
prey or an entire planet somehow, or the lovely
burst in the burning heart of the next god.

I call to the maker of visions, the one who has the power to exchange arms for wings, the one who pierces even obsidian with that one look, the one who often crawls up in dreams and helps to open the very shadows of trees on the wall so that I might enter another kingdom . . . as if I knew the Sioux ghost dance, a circle pounded into the cabin floor from last night's fury, stopping this morning to examine the sweat drawings she left on the walls, the million brush marks of her hair.

Once, I believed the river was a way in, the heart
a literal beating compass, the body a cache of
nightmares to be left behind, smoldering in a
burn barrel . . . now it is exactly what I never saw:
a way out, piercing the needle's eye of the soul, a
system of runs and eddies, a long, flowing lens,
existing finally as one chance to toss every word
written or thought in a last move to sneak out of
the skin, travel far, as far as necessary to see for
the first time how to mend that self, burned down
to what has been rendered beyond recognition.

No way in, no way out, the map tossed months ago, the mind fenced on three sides, the riverside open, listening to what some people call the chatter of a feeder creek . . . long ago the first language was born along with exploding stars, and now the ghost smoke of those ancient words drops out of the woods, mixes with water sound, but I cannot speak, and only listen, anxious for every hard silence I have known to be rounded, rendered harmless, sweet on the air as it leaves the tongue.

The aboriginal dog spirits rose up out of the creek
last night, brought their ancient instruments
and sang the world back down into the ground,
"starting over" they sang, the refrain making more
and more sense as the ground fell away and we
were all alone, our raging fire in the middle of
a new cosmos . . . I ate their songs all night, my
belly full of what might come with the next life,
the one that started this morning as they sang up
the sky, birds, animals, humans with better hearts
trickling in.

Every converging vortex on the wind map of the
world mistaken for swirling pain and anger, the
satellite hums and shakes, charting violent storms,
vast acres of wild sea, while down here, lights out,
I can smell the river steaming . . . so much for the
peace of flowing water at my feet, all around me
the night hunters ache for more, tree roots soak
in blood, and those skins left behind waiting for
their ghosts to limp them home.

Hard to believe the earth could turn so ragged so quickly, the sounds of a slow-motion implosion, everything falling into itself, even the angels must be rubbing their eyes, the hearts of men reduced down to blood dust, almost every river suddenly empty . . . tonight I fished under a half-moon, waded into a pool of moonlight and water, offered myself up to be dismantled, dissected beyond any memory of self, felt my blood turn to water, mind loosed and trailing off.

The half-moon behind a mottled sky, more like
an eye in a head full of light, expecting one of
the gods, or God himself, to drift in, straighten
every bent nerve on earth, relieve some heat in
our blood . . . this fever, moon fever, the way
the roiled lake sounds like a sea, how my skin is
more kite than skin, and those moons of Jupiter
humming somehow, as a probe passes by, bound
for a deeper black place, while down here, every
body churns in its own cauldron.

At first a koan, "What to be done?" then a mantra,
finally a prayer said into flowing water, because so
many things bleed, each individual kind of pain
like a fire coming in unseen from far off, then
the searing begins . . . "Where to go?" a haunted
voice probes, and tonight I choose not to enter the
river, afraid it has somehow turned itself over, the
bottom of rock, clay, sand, and gravel exposed
to the sky, no way to get through to water, and
nothing to be done about it.

Whether to say the dying of the night, night
falling, cover of darkness when the root cellar
of dreams opens its maw and you take that last
step into the wet dark, and the first of your bones
slides out into the soul lamp, where all your past
selves huddle around the marrow-fueled light . . .
but I take in the smoke, the haze of barely seeing
anything my entire life, the past an emptying
cistern, the future a single cloud just now passing
beyond an imagined horizon.

Long ago I crossed the last border, covered my tracks, and entered that place where new hearts float by daily in the river, the place where every secret known by every animal is revealed in each one of those hearts, and I tell you this, they are mine for the taking, and how pointed it has been to use a different one every day . . . the sky is not endless, and the universe collapses into a tiny point, beyond which is, as you suspected, a nothing, where, despite reason, there is another sky, and every world is a river, no banks, a place where I wear a disguise to appear as if I belong.

Tracing this unusual light over the river, light
pinks and yellows, dark clouds behind as if the
sky is about to mix itself into the color of a bruise,
or perhaps an actual bruise might manifest itself
just upstream, float down at treetop level to
drop its pain . . . I know there is more than one
fist behind the sky, the world punched close to
senseless, the moon representing the only clear
eye we are allowed to see, blinded by blood and
coagulated air, I feel one lung trying to become a
gill, the other just now dancing away outside my
chest.

So easy to build a wall out of river stones, lock the gate, commandeer the sky over this small place, call it a nation, not giving orders, merely taking them each day from the current, the roots of old willows, sure that I could read the future, however short, in the patterns of passing clouds . . . I renounce my place in the order of things, I turn from the world of human beings, and turn toward the old language of pure touch, as if I could chip my own bones for the tools to carry my heart in a basket made of woven hair, the words of her long, delicate fingers carrying light.

Every day a psalm, how it begins out of the past
and moves away so quickly, the sweetest parts
of each hour as if they were drops of honey or
whiskey falling from the trees, the path down to
the river illuminated only by the light of words . . .
these daily water chants recorded in a book bound
in the skin of sleep, how a dream weaves through
each day, sewn by the hands of the apparition
waiting at the edge of daylight to slide into the
bed where desire burns under the floor.

Soul and spirit head for the basement under
the basement where all my apocalyptic dreams
play like silent movies, their eyes splattered with
grainy light, comparing illusion to reality, finding
no difference . . . up here heart and mind find
that crevice in the body where the creature who
devours fear sharpens his teeth, and while the
basements rumble, he leaves by the back door,
guard hairs rising, enough blood in his giant heart
to get some work done.

Watching a clear sky, stars, that layer of darkness between me and the other world, and even though I hear it running alive below my feet, some nights this river moves as a river of tears, always trying to get to some other place, the memory of it gone even before it arrives . . . the world shifts toward entropy, as if all the ancient myths had coalesced around a single dying fire, the day's kill gone cold, every human heart slowing to its last beat, no one left to repeat the tale, even the gods gnawing at their own bones.

The sky almost obscured by a steady volume
of perfect clouds passing over the lake, the dog
stalking minnows, coming up empty every time,
while I drop another thought into what was
once a well of discarded wisdom, now, no doubt
bottomless . . . all these years clawing around for
the link between heart and mind, soul on the
edge shaking its head, now and then pointing up
at the sky, swirling water with its hand, doing
what souls do, bags packed waiting to leave.

Those cedar waxwings crossing over the river,
chasing insects, and in an instant their predatory
flight ends a life, but here, watching from the
creek deck, they split time when they cross flight
paths, the sky opens and I step through the veil of
right here, right now . . . I travel the distance from
my deck chair to infinity and back, hearing water
over rock as faint murmur, a message I already
know: stay low to the ground, keep your head up,
eyes tuned to the messages sent by the sky.

Autumn already forming high over the Canadian
border and the leaves beginning to turn, time
boils down to ash, dry brush, each bone feels
as if it is being backed out of my flesh, given
wings, and told never to return to this body, the
remnants of all the summers I have lived become
a diminishing fuel . . . I know my marrow is
headed for the sky, my skin left as a marker soon
enough, while around me, words I spent years
turning to ink, rattle away in the wind.

Watching rain, mist traveling downriver in a slow
wind, hunkered under cedars, I speak to the sky
and seek to be captured by grace, yield to the
sky woman I know is coming just for me, her
silk talons scraping the air toward my jugular, a
silent begging to be dismantled far upriver, then
put back together to heal these self-inflicted
wounds . . . the mid-August light yellows, settles
down in the field across the bend, if I stay awake I
might see this new version of myself dragging my
skin through the stubble, pause long enough to
nail it to a tree and never look back.

Today's reading opens up a vision where I watch my ancient soul being passed between immortals, held in each of their hands, the murmur of a primal language let loose in my veins, still trying to surface in this life, become an act of alchemy where water turns into words . . . which trail to hike, the ridge or the creek, one leads to a view of open sky, the other to a place where water seeps from the side of a hill, that one spot of all locations where the old ones came to drink, speaking their words into the dirt where they emerged to life as soul birds, flying off to roost in our hearts.

Feeling the world churning in its own blood, the
thought of entropy a dream, knowing the poles
will melt down, whole countries will disappear,
and the man who draws the maps will watch his
hair fall out drawing the last mountain range left
above the rising sea . . . I sit up high on the ridge
and look down through acres of high-canopied
trees, humming and singing to the dog with me
who couldn't care less about the damaged arc
of time, my hands have learned how to do a few
rudimentary tasks, use tools, write poems against
the grave, while my heart shifts and feels the wave
of final loss already forming in the tectonic plates
under God's skin.

That first slide into sleep, like ice on a griddle, following the songs of pagan women storming through the villages in search of satisfaction, the moon just rising, and no one cares, beds of straw moving inside hurricanes of pure abandonment, thousands of souls turned black on their way to a long perdition . . . I count my own blessings, wide awake, able somehow to hear the continents shift under my own bed, take the vow to settle up later, my body a vessel, a ship made of bones, sure I see a way to lose myself to those warriors moving like lovely scythes through the field where every blade of grass is made of longing.

Early September rain, the river rising, tucked up
under the eaves, reading the Psalms, so many
friends around me in peril, wondering what
the limits are to human suffering, the pages
of the book flaring up as if they were burning
holes in the dark, the trail of light signaling the
way out . . . somewhere, my ancient memory is
working its way out of my deepest cells, all the
old gods who left their whispered admonitions
have come back, their lips pressing against every
bruise, this body trying to rise, lean into the night,
certain there is some kind of peace out there I
have never seen.

Some tribes eat the ashes of their dead, some
monks perform sky burials, sending their brothers
off in a rush of dark wings, flesh in their beaks,
some of us just sit down, and though it looks
like we do, we never get up, almost bolted to the
ground where those we love listen to their spirits
sift through the soil as if it were sky . . . fire gone,
the ashes cold enough to eat, dry oak and ash
mixed with the bones of trout, one owl far off
gathering himself for a night of hunting, maybe a
chance to take this mix of magic char into myself,
drift off piece by piece, swept up, carried off,
white feathers vanishing into the woods.

What the day holds, cupped and offered up with
grace maybe, or something dark behind my
back that will bend trees, turn the heart against
itself, the sky ripped open into an endless wound,
every saint lining the way and the road toward
that unattainable shelter where silence once built
fires, wrote blood poems on the walls . . . long
ago I yielded my imagination to the elements,
knew water would do all the work, yet, I walked
dirt paths, built fires against sadness, knew that
beyond the ring of firelight I could take just one
step, leave myself behind, hoping that enough
brooding in the darkness would allow me to
grow a new tongue out of heart tissue and all that
flowing dream skin existing like air around my
body.

What heals, heals, and what doesn't never goes
away, the fist always visible inside the scar, or
how pure loneliness has so much of the memory
of pure joy pounding on the door, the heart's
passions being dragged outside and chained to a
post, all that wound licking to keep the tongue
occupied, swollen to twice its size, unable to
stop . . . once, in the pure darkness of loss, I
remember being trapped in the tiny closet my
life had become, tried to conjure a deal with the
powers, let me roll my skin up and light it like a
torch, maybe trade the few dry scraps of joy I had
left to keep on burning, miracles forming in the
shadows.

So I blaze with the alchemy of desire mixed in the mortar of regret, I burn away all the debris of the self, then pull out my flaming heart to make a sign in the night sky, writing the names of the people I love with flame and sparks, eating the embers as they fall into my mouth, hoping that the sack of my body might serve as a warning marker hung in a tree, signaling the place where you become a creature of pure abandon . . . at this altar of dried skin hung in a tree I leave a book to be written in, the journal of those who pass, who suddenly have the urge to cast their own bones, pull them out one by one, knowing that nearby in the woods, the old one who knows what the bones tell, points them on their way.

Just now an owl calling from above the cabin, a reminder that my mind is weak, wasting time on breathing in the dust of bad ideas, bad language, too many days lately of waking to a sky filled with clots, every cloud barely able to move past the trees across the river, ghosts and the ghosts of ghosts requesting that I hand over the keys, torch the pages stacked in the house, unravel even more of what is already unraveling . . . on the deck at the edge of the creek I punch into the dark sky, wait for a slow, fierce haymaker to come back, pound me up into the hills, give me one more chance to lie back, lick every wound I ever had, fall asleep with nothing around me that is human, no light in the overcast sky, the moon already gone.

We pass away, moving at first into our lives
and then out, all that time gathering light and
the seeds of a long peace we will grow into,
somewhere else where we will all find ourselves
again, changed beyond changed, and timeless,
and able finally to feel the universe inside of
us that was always there, expanding in every
direction, every dark corner illuminated . . . the
soul is a flame, burning a certain number of days
for each of us, so when we get to the last day, the
soul has learned how to burn outside of time
and space, fueled by its own grace and the pure
fuel of holy spirit, and that too passes, not away,
but hovers forever, burns and burns without ever
ceasing, burning everywhere, everywhere, the
light, everywhere.

I imagine the place to go to absorb the deepest loss, a place like a cave inside a deep well, a place where it is impossible to see, the darkness devouring the brightest flame, no sound but the constant drip of more and more darkness, and there, at the exact bottom you go to work . . . first, the hammer of anger strikes what is left of the heart, but the heart does not yield, instead, tool after tool takes up the work, the hammer of loss, and sorrow, and slowly, the hammer of light and peace slows into a delicate massage, the heart catching fire again in the tinder of what must be done to honor the light the dead pass to us as they leave us behind to do our most valuable work.

Woke to a mind tumid with so many errors, wrong turns, missed opportunities, a gathering ignorance of the actual gospel, all around me the gates beginning to close, never fully coming to terms with the vanishing number of days ahead of me . . . they say Indians sing songs of their own death, a celebration of sorts, the words becoming the actual exit ramp you walk out of this world, while I envision these dry leaves crackling under my feet singing me out in a different way, one path upward, carried off by wild birds, those ancient female spirits following the directions in their blood.

Waiting this morning for the one who sends
mercy to those who need it, not in small gestures
like a few more breaths, or one more sunrise, but
something large and grand, maybe a cosmic cloud
slamming the earth in one huge storm of mercy,
every pain and sorrow removed, scars of every
kind banned, erased forever . . . rambling out of
the cabin to a sky filled with light, bright healing,
every word from now on a prayer of gratitude,
knowing that all downriver, on every river and
in every place, we will feel our bodies lighten,
become loose, almost airborne, our lives turning
into living psalms, bones on fire, the next life
waiting out there for seeking.

Counting an infinity of river swirls, enough leaves
floating by to build a hermit's nest, figuring out
just how much rope I was given at birth before
I stumble to the end of mine, lantern out and
no fuel, the path gone into absolute darkness,
that place where you imagine creatures without
skin, bubbling chants out of their mouths, their
directions skewed, futile . . . stake me down
somewhere, build a wall of stone, burn everything,
record that glint of light in my eye, then cut me
loose, drag me close to the embers, swear an oath
to never mark this place on any map.

I need to take my own advice, follow strands of
lantern light deeper into the woods, sit down,
destroy the lantern, expose my chest to let the
night fliers in to feed, convince one of them to
carry off my heart, leave the shroud of my skin
as a false map for the way out, hoping someone
might track my spirit anyway, knowing it would
be waiting for her at the end of a bloody trail . . .
I count stars disappearing with the sunrise, the
moon an opaque husk, the river far below me,
sitting on the ridge where I pull the talons of last
night's dream messengers out of my neck, feel too,
the welts of kisses left as reminders, my skin still
steaming.

No chaos here, where one creek meets one river,
the trees dropping leaves all morning, and the
dog, stepping now and then to retrieve a leaf,
is momentarily lost in the falling remnants of
this vanished summer, which reminds me that
I want no part in the continued loss of days,
weeks collapsing behind me, the future a dark
blue black the color of a deep bruise . . . to be
caught out in the open in this feral culture, where
even the stones could be hostile, is a lesson in
shape-shifting, moving from shadow to shadow,
changing skins in midair, man to otter, back to
boy, then water rat, looking up at the perfect order
of the clouds, that lovely sound I wish I might
hear of the world, soft-creaking to a full stop,
locked into here, now.

Late October, the first snow and the moon
disappears, so I open every window in the cabin
and let the darkness into the rooms, run my
fingers through the thickness of it, no ambient
light, slowly shedding a skin hardened by August
heat, as if I might drift up through the roof,
become an angel, naked but rising too, riding out
of here on the thermal of my last breath . . . but
morning light settles back in, signs outside near a
smoldering fire that a covey of drunken renegade
saints came through in the night, looking I
suppose, to take a spiritual scalp or two, a few
knives left in the wet ashes, abandoned pages of
psalms torn out of my Bible, posted everywhere
on the trunks of trees, and their warning still
echoing back from hours ago, to live the rest
of my life on my knees, else I face their return,
become just one more scalp flapping against a
sinner's pole.

At first the desire to read that book about the remote islands of the world, the ache for less and less, a hut made of a downed reconnaissance aircraft, a bowl made from the pilot's skull, my skin aging prematurely, something close to papyrus, where I would, of course, write my memoir in my own blood . . . but I want to wear this day as a tattoo, never leave this place, carry it that close to my skin, packed in here against a wall of earth formed by the glacier eleven thousand years ago, and that glacial till, pebbles I roll in my mouth, a hedge against the thirst I carry, hoping the diviner, the water witch might find me with those lovely dousing rods she has made of her legs.

Nothing moving in the dead grass across the river, but the wind is there, and all those beings we cannot see, as if we were all prisoners behind glass sitting inside some museum diorama of what once was, but will be no more, our prayers unanswered and tossed off God's plate because he has left for a long rest from such horrible labor . . . every cloud passing has somehow been the same shape for hours, a gray mass, floating tumors in a blue sky, another sign that he does not linger but is somewhere washing up, the debris and grime of centuries gone down a drain too large to imagine, mumbling to himself, no evidence anywhere of what once passed for human intelligence, and the new clouds he conjures become a better breed of angels, their wings longing for the memory of warm skin, men who once knew things.

If only: the soul's palms could turn the mind
small enough to make of it a pebble, send it out
of the mouth and down the path, kicked on a
walk, kicked again and then abandoned, and the
mindless body headed toward a small fire on the
bank, where it might find itself at rest, fog rising
off the river and the trees dripping snowmelt,
with nothing to be made sense of, not even
the sky which is so gray the horizon cannot be
seen . . . dinner, and I sit by the fire, eating fog,
bowl after bowl, but nothing fills me, then more
bowls and finally I open my chest and let the air
fill me, fattened on nothing, lying stretched out
looking up at a blank sky, so dense that I will
never find the right star to guide me out of this
place, body ragged and weary without a compass,
night coming, made of more nothing, that black
nothing, hearing its cape caught only for an
instant up in the high trees.

Each day is an empty bowl, a poet I've forgotten
once told me, and today I placed mine outside,
filled it with water, and hovered over it, waited
for the sky to reflect into my eyes, but nothing
happened, only my aging face staring back rippled
by wind now and then, and then the sky came
in, low and gray and the bowl was low and gray
and my face was low and gray and I remembered
reading about people who could conjure the
clouds as portents, the future already up there
and rolling past, out of sight way too soon . . .
the tongue is a miracle as is the heart, and those
two together work as a broom in the mind, loss
mingled with dust, regret caught in the throat as
I try to sing it out of myself, counting up the days
to another birthday, while up above me, the sky
breaks open and that one cloud moving due east
gone before I was able to decipher what it said.

Partially lost in a snow squall up high in the hills, and the late afternoon Advent light somehow amber, and I long to find enough pine resin to coat myself, lie down in the cold, and pray to be found centuries from now, propped on my knees facing the light, thinking a last thought before entering the frozen silence, how I might enter the void before it was a void, pure light in God's mind . . . grateful for having been made, happening to turn up on earth at this time, and now longing to stop right here among trees, close by the river, even closer to the creek moving below me like a dark, open vein, only the desire to trade my blood for that other blood, hunkered like a pilgrim on the road, anxious to trade my life for whatever endless fever I am offered.

What would I do with the bodily relic of a saint,
the birthmark stolen from an ancient master, or
that eyelash a wandering pilgrim in Ohio claims
was secreted away from the rising body of Jesus,
held up, she claims, on every new moon to light
her way, glowing like a miniature sun she carries
in a perfectly clear ink bottle, all light and no
heat . . . each petition slides off my lips and hovers,
hummingbird-like, in the heavy air hanging over
the river, moves off to help heal the loved ones
who are suffering right now, and I like to think,
how they might sense the slight movement of my
air prayer as it passes through them, travels to a
divine ear some other believer has housed in a
bell jar, a believer who is just now uncovering that
perfect ear near a feeder creek, knowing the rattle
of water language is always doing its holy work.

All those sad priests gathered around a meager
fire up behind the ridge, trying to say the name
of God, chanting that something even close to
his name might rise up in the insignificant smoke,
their firewood wet, no tinder and a collected
experience of lighting only matches, hundreds
of candles and no heat to speak of . . . while next
to me, two fierce, ghost warrior maidens have
passed through the walls, offered their bodies
to the woodstove, igniting their cloaks and
breastplates using only the fire in their bones and
their luminescent swords: left behind for me to
use them in the morning to cut myself loose from
the restraints they thought they needed to extract
what they desired.

The heart half submerged in a kind of sargasso sea, awash in the debris of the high or low cost of living, the ghost echo of mythology lodged in the veins, how to fashion a shroud from river water or these huge trees surrounding me, neither fortress nor dungeon, only trees, growing into the light, that empty sky space that surrounds everything, covers pain and loss, as if it were some kind of powerful skin . . . I nod to the compass points, then to the vertical position of where I am, my woods littered with the hides of countless selves who have slipped past the border of being into deeper being, no heart, only the steady thrum of current, that constant sound of my soul hammer pounding my shadow onto the bark of a dead ash, as if it were some kind of sign, a plan for merging with the collective mind of roots, underground streams, only to vanish in weather, cleansing rain, not even a memory circling, swirling in itself.

I bent the day into myself, bent light and memory
and time, which immediately abandoned itself
to the past embedded already in the future, and
later, I channeled the light from the stars into
the funnels of my eyes, and here beside the river
I cursed the black coals from a hundred fires and
then took them into the cabin, mixed them with
blood and creek water, a vial of sweat saved from
a day when I pounded cement with a hundred-
pound air hammer, remembered how I dreamed
myself out of that concussive mantra into the
arms of the creature who haunted my dreams
back then . . . so, on a humid late August day, I sit
in a chair on this deck, watch my sweat bead, and
then take the slow path to the creek, evaporating
within inches, no work now, no fishing, only the
way I push a memory out into the haze to see
if it can survive my fierce assault once it grows
wings, hovering like a magic bird, filled with the
weightless melancholy of lust, then wheeling away,
disappearing as if eaten by the sky.

Apparitions all day, part rain, part flesh, the scarce light under a dome of thunderclouds, where something is singing to me beyond sight, how the cumulus rolls and climbs, tossing whatever it is up there into a deeper song, lines written in an ancient soul language, filtered through lips which most certainly know how to encircle a life, bring it back to breathing on its own, the maps of the future torn to tinder, fire already in her hands . . . thinking in this waking/half-waking dream that the river pauses, nothing moves past, but I hear my breath as though coming out of a tunnel, the river silent and clear and somehow solid, magic dripping all over me from those raging clouds, ghost disguised lover, speaker of conjoined languages, tongues moving over skin, writing those words you can barely read, following their arc to a place where all things gleam, mean something other than what they are.

A long night, trees falling, dead ash, bark gone
and the trunks picked clean, enough to mean
that if my thoughts were slow birds they would be
caught in the sweep of branches, fluttering against
the ground as if it were some kind of dense sky,
the moon waning, a prayer or thousands of them
uttered out of the lungs, how each one leaving
sounds like feathers brushing silk, writing a single
invisible word as it passes . . . so I cover trails in,
mark false ways, and piss against rocks to widen
the spray of marking this place, heart pounding
uphill, I stop to watch my veins pulsate, sure
there is a voice in my bloodstream that knows
every folk song made by bloody hands, the secret
tongues of dying animals, how the clouds speak
the future where I might trade this dark marrow
for a single bag of light.

River brown as ground, no leaves, no food to
feed that "idle lust of my eyes" my dear friend
referenced so long ago, reminding me that even
in the starvation light of December I have those
June nights eddying, and return often to that feast
of memory, as if I were once again with those
coyotes running the high ridge, stopping in the
dark to snarl down another bite of wild heart, the
faint light etched like a tattoo across my naked
back . . . so the tongue knows how to feast on
more than words, meat and blood, knows the
literal landscape of caress, the arc of leg and wild
sinew up against a lip, the sweet imprint of bone
against skin, the only flaw in the night, when
time drags the carcass of the past into the light.

A morning of snow devils churning across miles
of ice and snow, the sun almost invisible, and out
here in the wind, I feel the moon under the earth
bending its faint reflected light toward another
morning elsewhere, knowing there is no fire large
enough to warm the soul's deepest reach, a place
where this brutal cold in my head pounds against
an ancient anvil made of frozen bone . . . what
to do when the blood seeks darkness, the body a
sluice into more darkness, and the light coming in
through the transparency of an idea masquerading
as a life, the voice rendered silent and weeping
into itself, no way out, except the decision to bore
deeper, the heartbeat a slow growing echo, far
away, as if the soul had decided once and for all to
walk beyond any horizon.

The moon is over the river, in the river, current
mixing with moonlight, and I walk upstream,
dip a hand to remind myself I am in a body that
yearns for more but needs less, my lungs taking
in cold air and the scent of draining swamps,
deadfall rotting all around me, but the light sings,
if that's what you call watching it surge by, no
desire to leave this place where the sky is a holy
bowl of darkness . . . I imagine grief hanging like
tiny ornaments in the dead ash still left upright,
or grief as some sour fruit that no one wants to
pick, and then joy comes in on a north wind, the
sky alive and thrashing, coyotes far off just now
raising their throats into the chaos, as if their long
howls could stop whatever is coming.

The words breathing in the dark, far off from the cabin, those words I sense but do not know, yet, the ones that may or may not appear in this bruised line of language, the ones ready to speak of the things I cannot see, that immense swale I visit in dreams, walking through what feels like tall, thick grass, knowing it is really a slough of tongues trying to betray what they know . . . the beginning of autumn, yet heat and humidity, the river mottled with fallen leaves, water down, nothing much to do but everything to do, the catalog of the world narrowed down to how far I can see and how far I have yet to see, time and distance in their constant collision, the trees growing as I sit, their roots moving under me, their slight movement unknowable, aquifer a bed that heals and feeds, even in that constant darkness.

A bird shadow, but no bird, the field is grass and
weeds hip high, and the sky is solid blue, no
clouds, the wind barely a syllable in the trees, and
I am wondering what thing passed over me so
slowly yet wasn't there when I looked up, caught
a retina burn of my life condensed into that one
glimpse of shadow . . . a cell explodes, becomes
a dark shadow in the blood, like a cloud headed
north, up into the head where it gathers sleep as if
it were rain, then evaporates into the heart of the
imagination where one lost poem has stationed
itself, meaningless and desiring to stay that way,
shrouded, never to see real daylight.

Walking the meadow with the shadow of a slow-moving cloud, stepping out and waiting for it to catch up, then again, such a tempting trail to follow, the wind unlike any kind of straight line, imagining it to be an invitation to step off into something so reasonable in these times, following clouds, the weather always present, an omen passing above us every second . . . it's always either behind us or ahead of us we think, but it's always under us, right now, the shadow vanishing at high noon, the brief rest between heartbeats, the drummer in the forest stopping to listen to crickets, the river hard against rock, stacked up, then plunging off into the dark holes where the old stories are chanted by water spirits, blind and deaf, but filled with echoes, their fire turned to burning water, tongues blazing.

Earth, air, fire, water, belong to none of us,
existing as wild entities with as much telling
us that Jeffers knew what he was talking about
when he wrote of the wild god of the universe,
so it is that I feel the future already inside of me,
heart that was once a blown-out star, atoms of
smoking debris, then the spark of flesh, mind
awash in fresh blood, the sound of something
unimaginably fierce tinkering in a far off
basement . . . descending stairs, followed by even
deeper stairs, more after more, always stepping
into more darkness, the light of galaxies burning
above, memory of bright light, but the desire to
embrace its absence, so that once known, this life
will always hold the journey as even more sacred,
a soul hardened against what swings in, comes
without warning, the char of ash used to write it
all down.

What does each one of these days weigh, and how does a body careen through month after month of carrying these heavy bales of grief and loss, the mind growing into itself, the light of sunrises barely noticed, much less celebrated, as each day should be, words passed between the dead and the living to remind us of the grace of breathing . . . that one bird dropping from a murmuration, at first like a stone, but righting itself, rising away and vanishing, but holding for several seconds in a retina negative, black bird, white sky, the sun hollow as a skull, the air weighted, bird dissolving, then exploding back out into this blue sea of air again.

Hiking the creek-of-a-thousand-deadfalls,
gathering sticks along the way to use as a casting
off of dreams that have caused so much trouble,
the world so close to me, this small fire made
against havoc and death, the only permanence is
being here, now, in this place I have carved into
a hill, the water below my feet always traveling
away from me . . . waiting for coyote talk, though
they sleep all day, those wild voices so necessary
to cleanse the air of human breath, thinking that
this day, though I am awake, might be a kind
of dream where the skin splits and wondrous
creatures slip in to drop their amulets, carried and
handed down for centuries, praying that I would
recognize them for what they are: golden seeds
that none of us should be allowed to bear.

On the eve of my birthday/winter solstice/more light,
something barely visible but impossibly large rises
up out of swirling snow and cold, beyond anything
I've been preparing for all these years, hard to see in
the ache of ice, sounding more beast than human, a
jumble of misdeeds and transgressions shackled to
guilt, a howl spun up from some fissure in the soul's
bedrock, impossible to decipher beyond its singular
ability to slice into me so quickly . . . the lessons
offered up every day in the sky, ideas vague as
clouds passing, a vagrant mind wandering the skull,
lighting no fires to stay hidden on the trail, sleeping
in the murky light inside the body, wondering what
I should do with this empty journal carried like
a stone for decades, have I wiped my tracks clean
behind me, when do I stop to take up residence
where I might regard my past as though I were
watching words slide off the page, longing for the
collective memories collapsed in my blood to round
some ancient, dark curve, come back in one piece,
each particle of the past conjoined in some kind of
solid, luminous murmuration searing the black sky,
the scythe of it glistening with all it has cut its way
through, wanting only to walk again those immense
places it has wiped clean.

The grandfather in me searches the darkening
sky, so visible now through bare trees, while
the planets, the earth, all seething, each ocean
devouring whatever we can jettison, but this
shortening transit has lost little speed over the
decades, each day adding a bit of soul fuel to a
still wild heart . . . whoever it was that painted
the moon the color of my wife's breasts lurks
now outside this room where I release words as if
they were birds of prey, the light from something
feral glistening in the trees just off the deck, the
sky full black now, wind rising into what I want
to believe is an ancient chant, no words, but
something humming in unison with the charred
piston in my chest.

The last flies drag themselves over the deck, their incredible lightness burdened by age, the day's weak light not enough to keep them alive much longer, some lift off, briefly, the others probing the edges, while my arms, tired from cutting wood, feel more like roots than wings, the days behind me piled like so much scree, the days ahead, numbered, of course, but those days my eyes can't see, already riding thermals sent up by dead saints who tend their ancient fires . . . so the body carves its initials into the soul, or is it the other way around, the soul moving through the heart's chambers with a torch in hand, fire knife singeing its way to daylight, knowing there's no way back in, pulled by the desire to simply let what's left of a life roost somewhere, wander into the thickets time holds for us to rest, maybe hide, cloistered, watching the night sky for new stars, light sent out eternities ago, then abandoned.

Four eagles drop down from a gut-colored sky,
sit at the edge of the ice and wait, perfectly still,
their waiting summoning up a prayer in me
that they have arrived as more than good omens,
wanting them to become the feathered gods who
will rescue all of us, the miracle of their rising
transforming into beings who tear the truth out
of the living, stealing their lying tongues, leaving
their hearts behind as the stones they are . . . what
to pray and what to offer knowing the belly of
greed is never full, though the thought of trading
a life for a life is the same as planting a tree after
you cut one down; if only I could conjure up
miracles out of this first fire of the year, summon
the actual stillness of the winter woods into me,
the full, deep peace of a river that has known
where it's going for thousands of years.

Grief is not shed like a skin; you carry it a lifetime,
adding more, hoping that someday every layer
will turn transparent, the world transformed
through a lens formed over decades, finally
polished by the love of what we loved, dogs still
cradled against an arm, asleep, dreaming their dog
dreams of grace, beauty, yet the bone ache of their
leaving remains . . . the ghosts of four dogs now,
ever-prowling the river with me, their sprits grown
outside of this time, this space, released into the
next life as guides, seers who once lived on earth,
how they taught us to be, they rise away, but hold
in their rising, looking back to see if their lessons
will be learned, too soon on their way into the
burning stars.

Wading the river tonight, wondering why it is we aren't crushed by the weight of the stars, or at least bent in half, though we might be and not realize it, all of us disfigured over millennia, the sheer weight of billions of suns, the uncountable tonnage of simply being . . . eons course through us, ash and debris make us who we are, carbon spirits that absorb light, our tongues always struggling to get free enough to utter that one universal thought we think we sense but do not know, if only we could merge, fall into the kind of grace that time offers up, offering a drink from a cup that is always full.

One bird flying is just that, usually nothing more,
but today it becomes a last thought that needs
to find a better place to land, all trees and rivers
everywhere, the landscape a weaving of deep blue
current and a high canopy of black soil grown
into a heaven of leaves . . . the people of the
First Nations knew the healing power of magic,
their reality a blend of elemental knowing and
the deeper powers of the world in the sky, even
how it was possible to fly underground, wings
under them, but not, their eyes guided by living
constellations we have never seen.

Blood, weary and sifting like ash through the
marrow, flesh simmering on a bone fence, the
body ready to try one more time to lift off from
this shattered place, though even the wings, once
lighter than air, now sag under the weight of the
world's sorrow, the blind choirs on every street
corner hidden inside the human heart, even they
have lost their bearings, hymns tangled in the
branches where the mind once used to roost in
the dark . . . but I believe something will sing
us out of this swirling stew, that tomorrow or
the next day or the next, some wild spirit will
drift in unseen, turn the blood cooler, make our
hearts back into the cisterns they once were, how
long ago they held sweet rain, the singing spirits
washing out of clouds, each of us returned to the
joy of such lovely saturation.

How to open the body's wounds to healing,
even the deep scars hovering just above bone
undulating every night, or perhaps they are flying
inside the body, dark crows of pain that never
perch but use the insatiable black engines inside
them to wander the interiors we seldom inhabit,
outlined but never seen . . . one hand trailing in
the current, a kind of cold salve, the fingers loose,
feather-like, every sensation signaling through
my body, but those deep crows circling above the
immense sky I hold inside me, how long before
they see enough light to lure them out?

After the Buddha's body cooled down, his
disciples gathered the crystal pearls of compassion
and wisdom that had left his body, lucent beads
made of the sacred mind, fused with ash and bone,
the smoke of his pure consciousness entering
every lung within miles, birds of prey coming
back at night to scour the site I imagine later seen
as glowing, their holy talons disappearing into
a wild peace as they flew away . . . halfway up
the creek ridge I tend a small cathedral of trees,
askew, toppled by wind, their roots in the air,
part sanctuary, part storage room, each prayer for
twenty years marked by a river stone in the dirt,
the memory of each prayer rising always the same:
cupped in my hands, sent aloft, a bird made to
only fly once, toward one perch, toward that one
refuge where nothing is lost.

The sorcerer's trick is to shorten the distance between the self and the world, somehow bringing the actual sky into the mind, the river into the bloodstream, the fruit tree into the shelter of the heart, enticing the birds to live in the eyes, your own skin to enlarge enough to cover the earth like a tent . . . my hive is a cave where I eat the honey of my own thoughts, the wind rising outside the circle of cloistered ideas, a place where the ghosts of saints are stacked up at the door, their lanterns barely visible in the mist the aorta pumps out, and the long paths I walk every morning dissolve into the crush of trying to get somewhere, realizing that I am already there.

Decades spent trying to build a monastery in
the heart, rough terrain and a constant lack of
attention, head turned toward clouds and wind,
the river churning even in my sleep while the
dream hammers, try to pick up the slack, make
up for the nod always toward the honey of
desire . . . the books say I've shed hundreds of
skins, my body's compass needle worn down to
gossamer-thin, the shack inside me, small but tidy,
leaking roof, and a few faltering candles, though
the ladle waits for the monk I thought I was who
seeks the sweetest water.

Surrounded by this immense circle of green at the cabin, deep inside it, the wild, slow fusion of earth, sky, water, passing flowing seeps on a slow walk back from fishing, even the concept of one leaf is enough to send the brain wheeling off into the forest, suddenly seeing as a bird of prey does, a talon mind reaching out . . . sometimes this life feels ceaseless, the flow of it, constant but swirling up against my skin, but then an eddy, stalled surface current, the backwash unseen, roiling along underfoot, the river bottom there but not there as if stepping into nothing, an unspoken prayer, praising the spirit's yielding.

Somewhere, Jesus is walking a road so long it has no beginning, moving so slowly you can't tell he's headed this way, while on the journey, stars will be born and die, the universe might stop breathing from one step to the next, entire solar systems merging in his head, becoming raw cells ready to start over . . . this life, sometimes accompanied by cellos, other times ancient drums, unfolding out of itself, no maps ahead, only footfalls, weary to feel the hands of strangers who know the way, or those wondrous immortals who line the path but do not speak, their hands calm as doves, open, filled with light.

The body's tectonics, bone grinding away the flesh,
so many reasons to just lie down, stare into the
sky, and take up with the feral creatures of the
world, to pass away from the use of words and
thought, a heart wrapped only in the weather, the
four seasons, the simple yet labyrinthine rhythm
of one beat at a time, the movements of the
human world brewing up the nation's toxins, the
only refuge a head between the knees . . . I gave
up adjectives first, then body language, seeking
a kind of emotional inertia, immobilized and
reeking of the swamp-water camp where I hole up,
small yet bright pitch fires, ancient cedars casting
back and forth up in the wind, their roots slowly
rocking, my back soaking in the creak and thrust
of weather, the way time should be measured,
in sway and return, the arc of being sometimes
slowed to nothing.

A beloved friend writes to console me, saying "the streams of grief never run dry," my heart telling me to submerge and let it do the hard work necessary to keep breathing, the spirit inundated, floating in a bloody concoction of remnants of memories, growing through a childhood of always being near water, the clear depths suddenly closing down, darker water ahead, praying there is a shore, somewhere . . . for years I spent time building a mold to fit every desire, crawled in, felt my life tightening in on itself, happiness a fruit hanging by nothing in still air, years gone by now, the world's mysteries existing like a vapor inside each cell, no answers to be found, something like a heart curdling far off, beating itself into submission.

Walking through waist-deep pasture fog, my eyes
awash in a thin veil of mist, still carrying the
white dust of a moth fallen apart in my fingertips,
rubbing it into another universe, I suppose, or
back into this one, dust to dust to more dust, the
night coming on like every other one I've lived
through, the dark rim of the sky closing down . . .
my blessings counted with each step, a few fireflies
near my face, their tiny lights no match for the
lack of moon, but lights nonetheless, something
making and sending out light so close, and then
one in my hand, its slow pulse, a heartbeat, living
dust, my own slowing breath lifting it back into
the dark sky.

If only the heart could shed misery as a ginkgo
its leaves, sudden and complete, bare in the light,
then, to step through all of it and walk a path
back to the cabin, carrying absolutely nothing,
only the memory of leaves on fire, the smoke
trailing off, into the lungs of people who long for
the feel of a past without pain . . . I bring boughs
in around me, mostly pine and cedar, face into
the wind, a hut of sorts, my back against a huge
basswood tree, something in me wants to release
my name, my self, whatever tiny interior bird
houses my soul, send it all out into the growing
darkness, and let it begin to dissolve, only the
slight sound of its settling on a bed of dry leaves.

NOW THEN

Nick Bozanic

Up and off to the side of the ragged, dog-dug lawn in a copse of trees who seem to have wandered over there to keep one another quiet company, for want of anything better to do, a pair of weather-scarred Adirondack chairs, stationed on a plank platform overlooking a modest creek, as slight and fugitive as a shy girl tripping and skipping and chattering softly to herself before easing into a deep backwash at the base of the bluff, keep watch over the river as it rounds a bend a hundred yards or so upstream to slide murmurous and urgent toward them and then passes, at once ever-present and already gone for good, away. Take a seat. Take a seat and sit still. Wait now. Just wait. And listen. . . . listen to the roil and churn of the river, the water speaking the first words of a poem . . . "the river becoming a perfect book, poem gone as soon as it is spoken, raising no questions, the beauty of no answers. . . ." The Poet, sitting right there beside you, becomes utterly permeable, a passageway, a way in and a way out, perfectly passive, which is to say *attentive,* which is to say *receptive*—poised on the threshold, Janus-faced, greeting each moment's arrival with its luggage of stars and clouds, moon and rain, stone and leaf, hope and sorrow, now and then and yet to come, as if, heeding Rilke, he were saying goodbye.

"Attention, taken to its highest degree," Simone Weil so memorably insisted, "is the same thing as prayer. It presupposes faith and love. Absolutely unmixed attention is prayer."

Unmixed attention, attention untainted by the ego's appetites, by the will's refusals of all that Being offers. Attention as pure receptivity, "taking what comes like a drifting boat," as Han Shan coaches us, or like a trout holding itself steady in the current, waiting for its daily bread, for the miraculous manna of midge or mayfly, nymph or imago. And the Poet's receptive presence suffused with gratitude engendering praise, which is the very pulse of prayer, like the river itself, becomes song, a voice, the poem its arrested echo.

Stepping into this river, we enter the paradox of eternity, wherein the simultaneous concurrence of the *nunc stans*, the standing now or momentary present, and the *nunc fluens*, the ceaselessly flowing time of becoming, coincide, that realm where time does and does not stop. Where now and then—both past and yet to come—are one and the same. Where the gods, both great and small, abide.

What better place to pray?

I have read—have listened, rather—to these poems—no, this poem, this one song, this singular singing . . . the blood of the Poet turning "to water, mind loosed and trailing off . . ." again and again and miraculously it is never quite the same experience, as if each time I turn a page the words I've just read, of their own sweet will, reassemble themselves into fresh configurations of longing and loss, of loss and longing, like the river itself—"Once I believed," the Poet confesses, "the river was a way in . . . now it is exactly what I never saw: a way out . . ." Just as "every blade of grass is made of longing," so "'gone' comes off the tongue too often. . . ."

Listen, listen . . .

Lean in close to hear, here, the human heart, weightless as

owls' down adrift on the night air . . . listen, listen for "the slight sound of its settling on a bed of dry leaves."

Let us pray.

ABOUT THE AUTHOR

Michael Delp is the former director of creative writing at Interlochen Arts Academy, where he received multiple awards from the National Foundation for the Arts for teaching excellence. He is the award-winning author of several works of poetry, fiction, and nonfiction, including *The Mad Angler: Poems*. He is coeditor emeritus of the Made in Michigan Writers Series.

More from Michael Delp

Lying in the River's Dark Bed

The Confluence of the Deadman and the Mad Angler

A rollicking meeting of two wildly different yet incredibly similar personas: the Deadman in the shape and form of a trickster and the voice of an apprentice river shaman, the Mad Angler.

ISBN 9780814341988, $19.99 paperback

As If We Were Prey

A dark, lively collection of stories about men prone to foolishness trying to make their way in a modern world.

ISBN 9780814334775, $19.99 paperback

The Last Good Water

Prose and Poetry, 1988–2003

Return to nature and discover—or rediscover—the marvels of life and splendor amidst the Great Lakes.

ISBN 9780814331712,
$22.99 paperback

Under the Influence of Water

Poems, Essays, and Stories

A collection of moments—how time goes away on a river—and the more esoteric, spiritual aspects of fishing.

ISBN 9780814323915,
$18.99 paperback

Explore These Related Titles from Wayne State University Press

The Winds That Scatter
New and Collected Poems

Nubia Kai

The work of a lauded poet-scholar whose poems excavate the hidden treasures of human consciousness from the ruins of a tragic history.

ISBN 9780814353141, $24.99 paperback

Decoding the Hill of Dead Kings

Poems by Alex Vartan Gubbins

A vivid portrait of a life lived between two homelands and the conundrum of diaspora—feeling rooted here, there, and in neither place entirely.

ISBN 9780814352960, $19.99 paperback

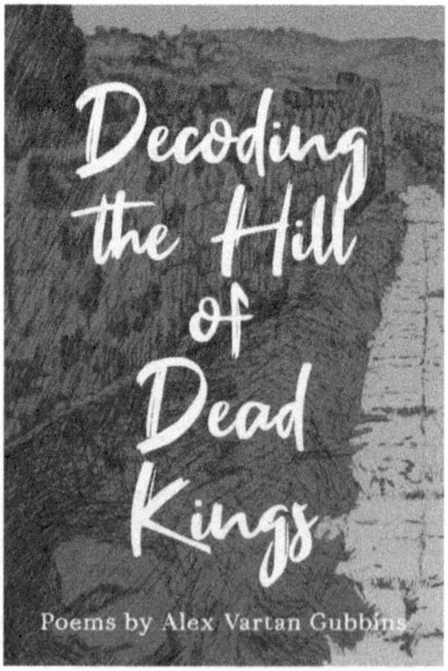